The Ruins of Mesoamerica

Duncan Searl

Newbridge
A Haights Cross Communications® Company

Before You Read

Imagine that you're hiking with a group of friends in the jungle, when suddenly you spot a piece of stone poking out of the ground. Curious, you begin to dig—and discover an enormous carved sculpture of a head. Sound impossible? That's just what happened to an archaeologist on an expedition in Mexico. His discovery helped open the door to the ancient world of Mesoamerica and the cultures of the Olmec and Maya peoples. As you get ready to read this book, think about the following, and make notes.

- What do you already know about Olmec or Maya cultures from books you've read or movies you've seen?

- Why do you think people study ancient civilizations? What can we learn from these civilizations?

Preview the book by looking at the table of contents, headings, photos, and special features.

- What do you see in this book that you already know something about?

- List three facts or ideas you think you'll discover in this book.

- Look at the photo essay on pages 24 and 25. Describe the kinds of ruins found at this ancient Maya city.

- Write down two questions you have about Mesoamerican cultures.

Contents

Out of the Jungle

The year was 1938. An American named Matthew Stirling was on a journey into the jungles of Mexico. Stirling was an **archaeologist,** a scientist who searches for objects from the past. He had come to this country to learn about the people who lived there more than 2,000 years ago. Stirling hoped to find ancient objects hidden in the leafy **rain forest.**

The archaeologist and his crew had already uncovered pieces of pottery and table-like **altars.** They began to dig up a large hunk of stone buried under the forest floor. Stirling thought the stone might be another altar. But as his workers cleared away dirt, they realized it was actually a sculpture of a giant head. It was magnificent, with thick lips and other strong features.

Matthew Stirling had seen pictures of giant stone heads before. Similar sculptures had been discovered in the area during the late 1800s and early 1900s. Archaeologists believed the heads had been

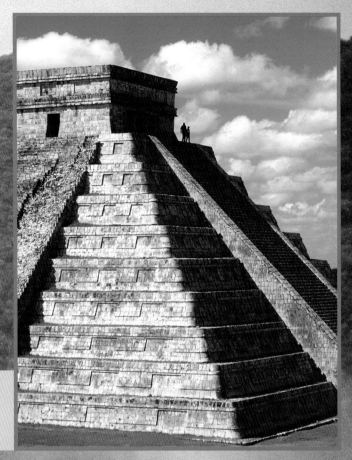

The ancient people of Mexico constructed cities with elaborate buildings, such as this pyramid.

carved 2,000 years ago. What they didn't know was who sculpted them, and why. They hoped that studying the stone heads would help them learn more about the ancient artists who had created them.

For archaeologists, ruins and the objects they contain provide important clues to the past. Old buildings, such as houses and temples, can show us where people lived and how they practiced their beliefs. Tools and other **artifacts,** or objects, can show us how they worked or prepared their meals.

Archaeologists piece all of these items together to understand what ancient people ate, what they wore, what they believed, and how they lived thousands of years ago. Without these clues, the past would remain a mystery that might never be solved.

Digging Up the Past

Decades after Stirling's discovery, archaeologists continue to explore Mexico and Central America to find ancient ruins. Each new discovery helps them learn more about the earliest people to live in this area.

Archaeologists use the term *Mesoamerica* to describe this part of the world. *Meso-* means "in the middle." So the word *Mesoamerica* defines an area roughly between North America and South America. It once stretched from northern Mexico into the

An archaeologist takes great care to lift a delicate artifact from the grave of an ancient king.

Archaeologists study ancient ruins on a coffee plantation in Guatemala.

Central American countries of Belize, Guatemala, El Salvador, and Honduras. The Mesoamericans who lived there came from different groups, but they had similar **cultures.** These groups lived during overlapping time periods, from 1500 BC to AD 1500.

This archaeologist carefully cleans the remains of a broken skeleton.

Searching for Mesoamerican ruins can be a real challenge. For one thing, ancient buildings and artifacts aren't easy to find. That's because a lot has happened in 2,000 years. The area's hot, wet weather has caused **erosion** and other kinds of damage. Over time, buildings that were once sturdy crumbled due to rain, wind, and the burning sun. As a result, there might be only a few buildings in an area where dozens once stood.

In this part of the world, nature can also be a problem. Rain forests cover many areas of Mexico and Central America. Over the years, these wildly growing jungles buried ancient structures under bushes, vines, and other plants. To find ruins, archaeologists have to pick their way through dense forests.

Once they know where ruins might be located, archaeologists put in a lot of hard work to uncover them. It can take weeks, months, and sometimes even years, to **excavate,** or dig up, artifacts and ruins. They must cut through forests and shovel dirt and mud. While they dig, they must also take care not to cause any further damage. The work can be backbreaking and tiresome.

Even with all these problems, archaeologists have made amazing discoveries. They've found buildings such as temples, pyramids, and royal palaces. They've also uncovered sculptures such as carved columns and the stone heads. And they've unearthed an enormous number of artifacts, including tools, cooking pots, and jewelry.

Who Were the Mesoamericans?

Every discovery that archaeologists make helps them learn more. They carefully study their finds and piece them together to uncover the mysteries of the Mesoamericans. As they work, they try to answer questions about these ancient groups. What were their lives like? How did they build such enormous buildings and sculptures? And what was the purpose of these structures?

So far, archaeologists have been able to answer some, but not all, of these questions. First of all, they know that Mesoamerican cultures came and went for 3,000 years or so. These groups included the Toltec, the Mixtec, and the Aztec. Two of the oldest cultures were the Olmec and the Maya.

The Olmec people lived in the area first, starting around 1500 BC. Archaeologists now know the Olmec were the

A Mexican farmer found this Maya city, named Kohunlich, in the 1960s. The jungle has continued to grow in and around the stone ruins.

The Olmec and Maya in Mesoamerica

Gulf of Mexico

Papaloapan River

Grijalva River

M E X I C O

Caribbean Sea

BELIZE

GUATEMALA
Motagua River

HONDURAS

PACIFIC OCEAN

EL SALVADOR

NICARAGUA

Map Key
Olmec heartland
Maya territory
Present-day borders

0   100   200 mi
0   100   200 km

ones who sculpted the stone heads. Before Matthew Stirling's discoveries, not many people had ever heard of this group.

It wasn't until ruins of an Olmec city were discovered in the 1930s that Stirling and other archaeologists began to put the pieces together. The ruins show that the Olmec were the first **civilization** to live in the area. That means the Olmec were the first to live in cities and the first to have an organized society with different kinds of workers. They were also the first to create great works of art and the first to build giant structures.

The Maya came later, around 900 BC. During their peak, thousands of people lived in and around Maya cities. One of the largest was known as Tikal. About 60,000 **residents** lived there.

Eventually, both groups deserted their cities. Over time, the rain forests closed in, covering the empty ruins. Nearby rivers played a part, too. They slowly deposited clay and mud into the area. After a thousand years, many buildings became buried under layers of mud several feet deep.

But the ruins that the Olmec and Maya left behind help paint a picture of life in the area long ago. Archaeologists work to learn more about these two groups because they created cultures that influenced those that followed. Their civilizations helped shape life in Mesoamerica for thousands of years.

This carving of a man carrying a child was discovered in La Venta. This ancient city near the Gulf of Mexico was built by the Olmec people.

9

A Conversation with an Archaeologist

Dr. Lori Wright is a professor at Texas A&M University. She teaches classes on the early Mesoamericans. She's spent a great deal of time in Guatemala and Belize exploring Maya ruins. Here's what she had to say about her experiences working as an archaeologist.

What kinds of ruins and artifacts have you uncovered?
As a student, I excavated ancient Maya houses. Now, I mainly excavate graves. I dig up skeletons to learn more about the health of the Maya. By studying their bones, I can find out the kinds of diseases they had.

How do ruins help you and other archaeologists learn more about the people of Mesoamerica?
Different ruins tell us different things. For instance, we can learn a lot about daily life by studying trash **middens**, or garbage heaps. Long ago, people got rid of broken pottery and other kinds of trash by sweeping them out their front doors. Over time, the trash collected into piles that are still preserved. Inside trash middens you can also uncover the remains of burned food. These remains show us what the Mesoamericans grew and ate.

Dr. Lori Wright

What are some of the problems archaeologists face?
Climate and geography are big obstacles. For the Olmec, some ruins are buried under a heavy layer of mud. For the Maya, tropical forests cover large parts of their **territory**. Transportation is difficult, too. Many of the roads are poor, and in some places there are no roads at all. When I was a student, it took me all day to reach one site where I was working. The first part of the trip was a 14-hour bus ride. That was followed by a two-hour boat ride. You had to walk for two more hours through the jungle. We needed to bring mules along to carry our equipment. The animals also carried back any artifacts that we found.

These archaeologists examine a Maya artifact buried in a king's tomb in Guatemala.

We've already found a lot of Maya and Olmec ruins. Do you think there's more to discover? There are probably a lot of smaller sites that haven't been uncovered. Sometimes, looters find these places before we do. They look for palaces that might contain riches to steal. Even if looters have stolen artifacts, archaeologists can still find out a lot of information from the everyday items that don't interest the looters.

Skeleton of a Maya woman

How do you find answers from the clues in ancient ruins?
We study people who live in the area today and who continue the traditions of their ancestors. Also, Spanish explorers who came to this region in the 1500s left behind letters and travel journals. They describe the lives of the people in the area at that time. Then, we look at any artifacts we find, and where they were discarded by the Maya. This tells us what activities they did and where they did them. We can put together those pieces with any new findings to get a complete picture of the Mesoamericans who lived long ago.

THE OLMEC

At dawn, an Olmec boy races to the river. He stops to watch dozens of men pull a raft bearing a giant stone. Weeks earlier, the men had traveled to mountains in the west to get the stone. To the boy, it looks like a black hill floating up the river. He will not see the stone again until the harvest ceremony. By then, sculptors will have shaped it into a fierce, yet beautiful, face.

Some archaeologists call the Olmec civilization the "Mother Culture of Mexico." That's because they believe this group had an influence on the cultures that came after, including the Maya.

The remains of Olmec buildings are some of the oldest ruins found in North America. That helps archaeologists know that this group built the first cities on the continent.

Ancient Olmec Cities 1500–400 BC

Gulf of Mexico

Tuxtla Mountains

Tres Zapotes

Papaloapan River

La Venta

Tonala River

San Lorenzo

Catzacoalcos River

Grijalva River

Usumacinta River

M E X I C O

PACIFIC OCEAN

GUATEMALA

Map Key
Olmec heartland
• City
— Present-day border

0   50   100 mi
0   50   100 km

These stone blocks are all that remain of an ancient Olmec tomb.

Their cities included San Lorenzo, La Venta, and Tres Zapotes. These three locations are **sites** in northern Mexico where archaeologists have now unearthed many Olmec ruins. They've discovered the remains of public buildings, royal palaces, and simple houses. Many of these structures were not found whole. However, there is still enough there to help archaeologists make guesses about life among the Olmec people.

Other structures that have been discovered include altars, temples, and pyramids made out of mounds of clay. All of these were probably used for religious ceremonies.

Preserved plants show that Olmec farmers grew squash.

Among the ruins, archaeologists have also uncovered the remains of food. The bits and pieces they found had been burned, which helped **preserve** them for all these years. From food remains, archaeologists have learned that the Olmec were farmers who mainly grew beans and **maize,** or corn.

This was an important discovery. In the 10,000 years before the Olmec existed, people had lived only as **hunter-gatherers.** They moved from place to place, hunting animals and gathering wild plants for food. Finding enough to eat took most of the day, every day.

Those early people didn't grow crops. There wasn't a lot of land that could be used for farm fields in the dense rain forests. But around 1500 BC, the Olmec discovered a technique that made it possible to plant crops. This discovery helped shape their culture.

Building a Civilization

Over time, the early Mesoamericans developed a farming technique called "slash-and-burn." They learned to slash, or cut down, jungle plants and burn them. This created a clear space for planting. The ash from the fires also made the soil fertile, which helped their crops grow.

Slash-and-burn farming made it possible for people to live in one place. They grew enough crops, so they no longer had to search for food. Around 1500 BC, the Olmec began to settle into permanent communities.

Farmers grew enough food to feed everyone in the community. That allowed other people to do different jobs. Some became artists, builders, or priests. In that way, the Olmec developed organized societies with several kinds of workers.

Some Olmec became sculptors. They left behind giant statues and tiny **figurines.** They also created **stelae,** carvings on flat stones or tall columns. And, of course, Olmec artists created the famous stone heads.

Although the stone heads all look very similar, if you study them closely you can spot differences among them. For example, the eyes have different shapes.

No one knows for sure why the Olmec carved these pieces of art. Archaeologists believe they were created to honor kings. Perhaps they were like our statues of leaders today.

Tools of the Trade
Pick - axes

Archaeologists depend on certain tools to do their jobs. The pick-ax is one of the most important. This sharp, sturdy tool makes it easier to break up tightly packed dirt and rocks. Along with a shovel, it's used to dig for artifacts buried below ground.

Some Olmec stone heads are as tall as nine feet and weigh several tons.

Archaeologists work to excavate an Olmec ruin in the ancient city of San Lorenzo. This column probably supported the roof of a temple.

Carved in Stone

Olmec artists used two kinds of stone: jade and basalt. Jade was used for figurines. Basalt was used for stelae and giant heads. By studying the surrounding land, archaeologists have learned that the Olmec had to travel great distances to find basalt. It was located in the mountains along the western edges of their land.

Getting the stone took a lot of work. The Olmec didn't have horses, carts, or machinery to help them. Instead, they relied on manpower. There must have been a huge **labor force** of workers to lift, push, and drag the stone from the mountains. They probably needed hundreds of people to get the job done.

Olmec workers traveled to the Tuxtla Mountains to search for basalt.

Archaeologists have experimented with simple tools and methods to figure out how the Olmec moved a heavy chunk of stone. Most believe a team of workers first searched for the basalt. Then they hacked out a piece with stone tools. Next, they dragged it

This Olmec tomb was built with basalt. It would have taken workers quite a while to cut and shape these thick, heavy blocks.

to the river on rollers made out of logs that were attached to ropes. After that, they loaded the stone onto a raft. Finally, they sailed back to the city. It would then take months for a sculptor to carve the stone into a work of art.

Sculptures are the few Olmec ruins found in one piece. Other structures have been damaged by the hot jungle climate. Some have also been buried. Over thousands of years, nearby rivers slowly deposited clay and mud, covering most of the buildings. Archaeologists believe they're now eight feet or more underground.

Many structures became buried naturally over time. But it appears the Olmec also buried some on purpose. At one ancient city, they rolled stone heads into a deep ravine. Today, no one knows the exact reason why they did this.

One thing we do know is that the Olmec abandoned their cities more than 2,000 years ago. The most likely reason is a drop in the food supply. Slash-and-burn **agriculture** had at first allowed the Olmec to build their civilization. But this technique weakened the soil until it became too difficult to grow crops. That meant there was no longer enough food. Rather than starve, the people left.

Many mysteries about the Olmec may never be solved. But archaeologists will continue to search for answers.

THE MAYA

At dusk, a Maya priest climbs to the top of a pyramid. Carvings on the steps bear the names of his father and grandfather. Like him, they were priests. They, too, once climbed these steps on ceremony days. At the top, other leaders stand waiting. Some wear snake masks. Others have feathered headdresses. As the priest reaches the top of the pyramid, the others bow. Together, they enter the temple to begin a ceremony.

By 400 BC, the last of the Olmec cities had been deserted. The Olmec people traveled to other areas to build new homes. Some headed east, to areas where the Maya people already lived. The Olmec probably shared some of what they knew about architecture and construction with their new neighbors.

The first Maya cities appeared around 900 BC in the **lowlands** of Guatemala. Over the next 1,500 years, the Maya spread north and west. By AD 600, their cities stretched across large parts of eastern Mesoamerica.

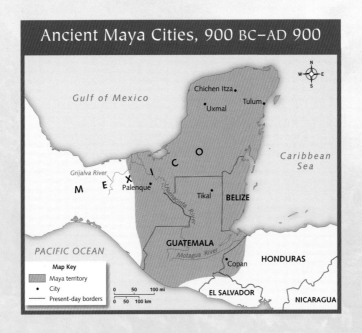

Ancient Maya Cities, 900 BC–AD 900

Gulf of Mexico

Chichen Itza

Tulum

Uxmal

M E X I C O

Caribbean Sea

Grijalva River

Palenque

Usumacinta River

Tikal

BELIZE

PACIFIC OCEAN

GUATEMALA
Motagua River

Copan

HONDURAS

Map Key

Maya territory
City
Present-day borders

0   50   100 mi
0   50   100 km

EL SALVADOR

NICARAGUA

Archaeologists have located the remains of several of these cities. They have also discovered more Maya artifacts than Olmec remains. Maya ruins weren't buried under river mud because they were in a different area.

Like the Olmec ruins, Maya structures can tell archaeologists a lot about life in ancient Mesoamerica. For instance, they know that thousands of Maya lived in these cities.

To build their cities, the Maya used a few materials that were different from the ones used by the Olmec. Instead of basalt, the Maya relied mainly on limestone and sandstone. They dug huge pits to get both kinds of stone. With these and other materials, they built pyramids, palaces, platforms, monuments, and temples. They also built ball courts for playing games.

Unlike Olmec structures, many Maya buildings are still around today. This palace is in the ancient city of Palenque.

Building from the Ground Up

From the preserved remains of food, archaeologists know the Maya were farmers like the Olmec. The Maya depended on slash-and-burn agriculture, too. But they also drained water from swampy areas to create farm fields.

The Maya grew beans, squash, and maize, just as the Olmec did. Maize, in fact, was their most important crop. One of their gods was the Maize God. The Maya believed that prayers to this god brought plentiful harvests.

Like the Olmec, Maya farmers grew enough food to feed a large **population.** That made it possible for other people to take on different kinds of jobs. Many became artists, merchants, soldiers, or priests.

Other Maya became builders. The most impressive ruins that they

An archaeologist works to restore damaged ruins at the Maya city of Uxmal.

left behind include tall pyramids. Most pyramids were made of limestone. They usually had flat tops and were built with several levels. But each pyramid had a slightly different shape that made it unique.

Archaeologists believe there were several steps in the building process. First, workers placed rollers beneath blocks of limestone to make them easier to move. With long poles, they guided the stones along the rollers and shifted them into place. Then they used ropes and pulleys to stack the heavy stones, one on top of the other. Finally, they cemented the blocks together with a thick layer of plaster. With smaller stone blocks, workers built steps into the pyramid's sides. A small temple was often constructed at the peak.

This sculpture shows the Maize God. The headdress represents an ear of corn. The hair represents corn silk.

Tools of the Trade
Trowels

During digs, when archaeologists are close to uncovering ruins, they must put aside pick-axes and shovels. These sharp tools might harm any objects they hope to find. At this point, a tool known as a trowel comes in handy. It's used to carefully scrape, slice, and clear away soil to reveal what lies beneath.

Archaeologists in 1933

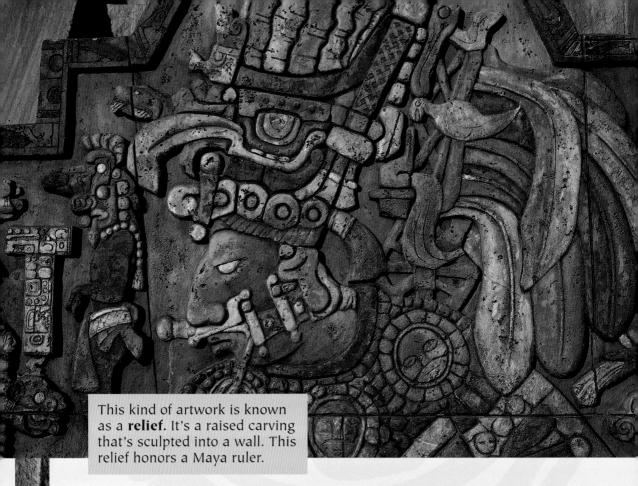

This kind of artwork is known as a **relief**. It's a raised carving that's sculpted into a wall. This relief honors a Maya ruler.

Life in a Maya City

What was life like in an ancient Maya city? Ruins show that most people lived in small houses. Their neighbors were usually members of their extended families—grandparents, uncles, aunts, and cousins. Their houses were grouped together around a small courtyard for all the members of the family to share.

At dawn, everyone got up and went to work. Many men worked in the fields, planting and harvesting hundreds of acres of crops every year. Others worked on building projects. They cut stone or helped build structures. Some men were artists who made colorful carvings and detailed sculptures. Others were soldiers who protected the city from outsiders. Meanwhile, women cooked the meals, made clothes, and fetched wood and water. There was no end of work to do.

Stone ring

Ball games were **sacred**. They were played in honor of the gods. Every part of Maya life had its own god or goddess, including farming, cooking, weaving, and sports.

Play Ball!

The Maya didn't work all the time, however. On holidays, they gathered in plazas and courtyards for religious ceremonies. Priests in costumes and masks conducted the festivities.

Part of the ceremony might be a ball game. Most Maya cities had ball courts, which were usually flat, with walls on either side. The courts were also narrow, less than 20 feet wide. That's less than half the width of a basketball court.

The Maya ball game was like basketball mixed with soccer. The object of the game was to hit a ball through a goal. Sometimes the goal was a stone ring or hoop that was placed at the top of a high wall. Two teams of players could knock the ball directly into the ring or bounce it off a wall. But they couldn't touch the ball with their hands or feet. They could hit it only with their elbows, knees, or hips. Although it was made of rubber, the ball was usually hard and heavy. So players wore padding to protect their skin from bruises.

A Visit to Chichen Itza

Chichen Itza is one of the best-known ancient Maya cities. It was founded around the sixth century AD and was once a center of trade. Let's visit some of its amazing sites.

The Caracol
The Maya used this building to study the stars. It has several small windows that were used to keep an eye on the sky.

The Plaza of the Thousand Columns
Carvings on the columns describe the great deeds of warriors. Actually, the name isn't really correct. There are only 200 columns.

The Temple of the Warriors
This temple was one of the last buildings constructed at Chichen Itza, before the Maya civilization began to decline.

Serpent Sculptures
Snake head sculptures are found throughout Chichen Itza. This one honors the feathered serpent god, Kukulkan. He was worshipped by all the ancient Mesoamericans, including the Olmec.

Stargazing

Some Maya structures show that they were interested in **astronomy.** They believed the gods controlled the sun, moon, and stars. So they built **observatories** to study the sky.

Many of their structures were also constructed according to the position of the sun in the sky. A temple in the city of Palenque is a good example of this. In December, on the shortest day of the year, the sun sets near the temple's roof. The fading afternoon light enters a doorway in the temple. The sunlight then disappears down a stairway into a tomb below. The Maya believed this process helped the old sun to die and a new sun to be born in the coming year.

A pyramid in Chichen Itza does something similar. It happens during the spring and fall **equinoxes.** On those two days every year, day and night are the same length of time. During each equinox, the sun shines onto the pyramid. A shadow begins to form. It creates an image of a snake. The Maya greatly admired this shadowy image. To them, the serpent was an important god.

To keep track of the changing seasons, the Maya used two calendars. One was like ours. It had 365 days and was based on Earth's orbit around the sun. The other was a 260-day sacred calendar. Priests used it to schedule planting, harvesting, and religious ceremonies.

Tools of the Trade
Soft Brushes

Cleaning artifacts requires a lot of care. One wrong move and an archaeologist could permanently destroy a delicate ancient object. Brushes are the perfect tool to handle this job. Here, an archaeologist uses a brush to gently clear dirt off a painted mummy.

This pyramid, called El Castillo, has 365 steps—one for each day of the year.

Leaving the Cities

Beginning around AD 900, the Maya began to desert their cities. Archaeologists believe they fled from attacks by other groups. Or, they might have left because of a drought or because they wore out their farm fields as the Olmec did. As the Maya traveled into other parts of Mesoamerica, they shared their culture with different groups.

Although their cities stood empty for a thousand years, many buildings remained. They have weathered some damage over time, but they may very well be standing in another thousand years.

MESOAMERICA TODAY

Mesoamerica is now Mexico and some of the countries of Central America. Many Maya continue to live in the region. There are now about eight million of them in Mexico, Guatemala, and Belize.

The Olmec also have **descendants** who live in the area. However, this group now goes by a different name. They are known as the Totonac people. Their language and other parts of

In the hills of Guatemala, Maya merchants sell pottery, clothing, furniture, and other kinds of artwork.

their culture are different from those of their ancient **ancestors.** Over the years, their way of life changed as they came into contact with other Mesoamerican groups. Even so, the Totonac people are proud of their ancestors.

Today, the Maya who live in Mexico and Central America keep their culture alive. Many still speak the language of their ancestors. Some live in cities. Others reside in small towns and villages. They farm the land as their ancestors did, growing maize, beans, and squash.

This Totonac man plays a small drum and flute.

Sometimes, though, they travel into the modern cities built throughout the region. They head into Cancún, Mérida, and other places to sell their crops at markets or to attend celebrations.

Meanwhile, many tourists head into the jungles to explore the ruins where the Olmec and Maya once lived. Millions travel from all over the world every year to tour these sites.

Today, many Maya continue to live in the region. Some enjoy wearing traditional clothing similar to what their ancestors wore.

The ruins are also important to archaeologists. They continue to study them for clues about both cultures. They want to learn as much as they can about life in the ancient Olmec and Maya civilizations. So they look for new sites and continue to explore old ones. Who knows what secrets these ruins might one day reveal?

Keep Going!

Here are some ways to share what you've learned, find out more, and develop your talents. Maybe you'll come up with your own idea.

THINK AND WRITE

⚜Imagine that you've jumped in time to the year 3011. You're digging in a place that was once someone's backyard. Suddenly, you come across a large plastic object with a blank screen and several buttons. What do you think this object is? Write a letter to a local newspaper describing your discovery. Explain how people might have used this object more than a thousand years ago. What can it tell you about life in that community long ago?

DIG DEEPER

⚜What questions that you had before you read the book are still unanswered? What new questions came up in reading? You can start looking for answers at these Websites. Write down your answers and tell where you found them.

Mesoweb
www.mesoweb.com/welcome.html

The Art, Culture, and History of Ancient Mesoamerica
www.ancientmexico.com

UPDATE

⚜Use the Internet or the library/media center to learn how the places featured in this book have developed and changed, and how they've also stayed the same. A suggested Website is:

Maya Adventure
www.sci.mus.mn.us/sln/ma/top.html

AN ARCHAEOLOGICAL FIND

⚜Picture yourself on an archaeological dig in a place of your own choosing—such as a rain forest, a desert, or a mountainous area. You and your team have uncovered an ancient city! Draw a map of what you have found. Does your city have pyramids? Palaces? Temples? Courtyards? Be sure to write captions to accompany the drawings that describe your discoveries.

GLOSSARY

agriculture \a′ gri kəl chər\ *n.* the science or practice of growing crops

altar \ôl tər\ *n.* a table or other kind of raised structure used for religious rituals

ancestor \an′ ses tər\ *n.* a person in your family who was born long before you, such as a parent or grandparent

archaeologist \är kē ä′ lə jist\ *n.* a scientist who studies the remains of ancient cultures

artifact \är′ ti fakt\ *n.* a man-made object used in everyday life, such as a bowl or a piece of jewelry

astronomy \ə strä′ nə mē\ *n.* the study of heavenly objects, such as planets or stars

civilization \si və lə zā′ shən\ *n.* a group of people that forms a community with its own system of government, religion, and learning

culture \kəl′ chər\ *n.* the way of life of a group of people, including their beliefs, holidays, music, and food

descendant \di sen′ dənt\ *n.* a person in your family who was born after you, such as your child or grandchild

equinox \ē′ kwə näks\ *n.* one day in spring and another in fall when the sun crosses the equator. On those days, night and day are an equal length of time.

erosion \i rō′ zhən\ *n.* the process of slowly wearing away by water, wind, or ice

excavate \ek′ skə vāt\ *v.* dig up

figurine \fi gyə rēn′\ *n.* a small carved or molded statue

hunter-gatherer \hən′ tər ga′ thər ər\ *n.* a person who fishes, hunts animals, and gathers wild plants for food

labor force \lā′ bər fors\ *n.* a large group of workers

lowland \lō′ lənd\ *n.* an area of land that is close to sea level

maize \māz\ *n.* a Native American name for the corn plant

midden \mi′ dən\ *n.* a small pile or heap of garbage

observatory \əb zər′ və tor ē\ *n.* a building or place that is used to study the sun, moon, planets, and stars

population \pä pyə lā′ shən\ *n.* the number of people who live in an area

preserve \pri zərv′\ *v.* keep safe or free from harm

rain forest \rān′ for əst\ *n.* a forest that receives at least 100 inches of rain per year

relief \ri lēf′\ *n.* a raised carving that has been sculpted onto a wall or other flat surface

resident \re′ zə dənt\ *n.* a person who lives in a particular place

sacred \sā′ krəd\ *adj.* relating to religious beliefs or worship

site \sīt\ *n.* a place. An archaeological site is a place with buildings or artifacts left by people long ago.

stela \stē′ lə\ *n.* a stone column or monument that is usually carved with pictures or writing

territory \ter′ ə tor ē\ *n.* an area that belongs to and is run by a government

---

Pronunciation Key

\ə\ **among** \ər\ **murder** \a\ **ask** \ā\ **ape** \ä\ **hop, car** \ch\ **chop** \e\ **end** \ē\ **greasy** \g\ **get**
\i\ **hid** \ī\ **ice** \j\ **jet** \ŋ\ **king** \ō\ **no** \ô\ **saw** \oi\ **toy** \oo\ **book** \ou\ **out** \th\ **thank** \th\ **then**
\ü\ **boot** \y\ **you** \zh\ **Asian**

Index